When He Whispers Your Name

Original photography by Kelly Meagher

ISBN 978-1-0880-3393-7 (hardcover)

Author's note: While Scripture is referenced throughout these meditations it is the author's understanding that most Scripture used is widely recognizable as Scripture and for the sake of poetic art, such references are not marked. Creative license to paraphrase Scripture has been taken, and is most notable in the 22nd poem where the majority of the stanzas are direct quotes of Scripture or paraphrased Scripture with no intention to claim such phrases as the author's personal work save for the combining of said Scripture into poetic form.

Cover Photograph: by Nine Koepfer

When He Whispers Your Name

Contemplative Poetry and Prose for the Spiritual Soul

Kelly A. Meagher

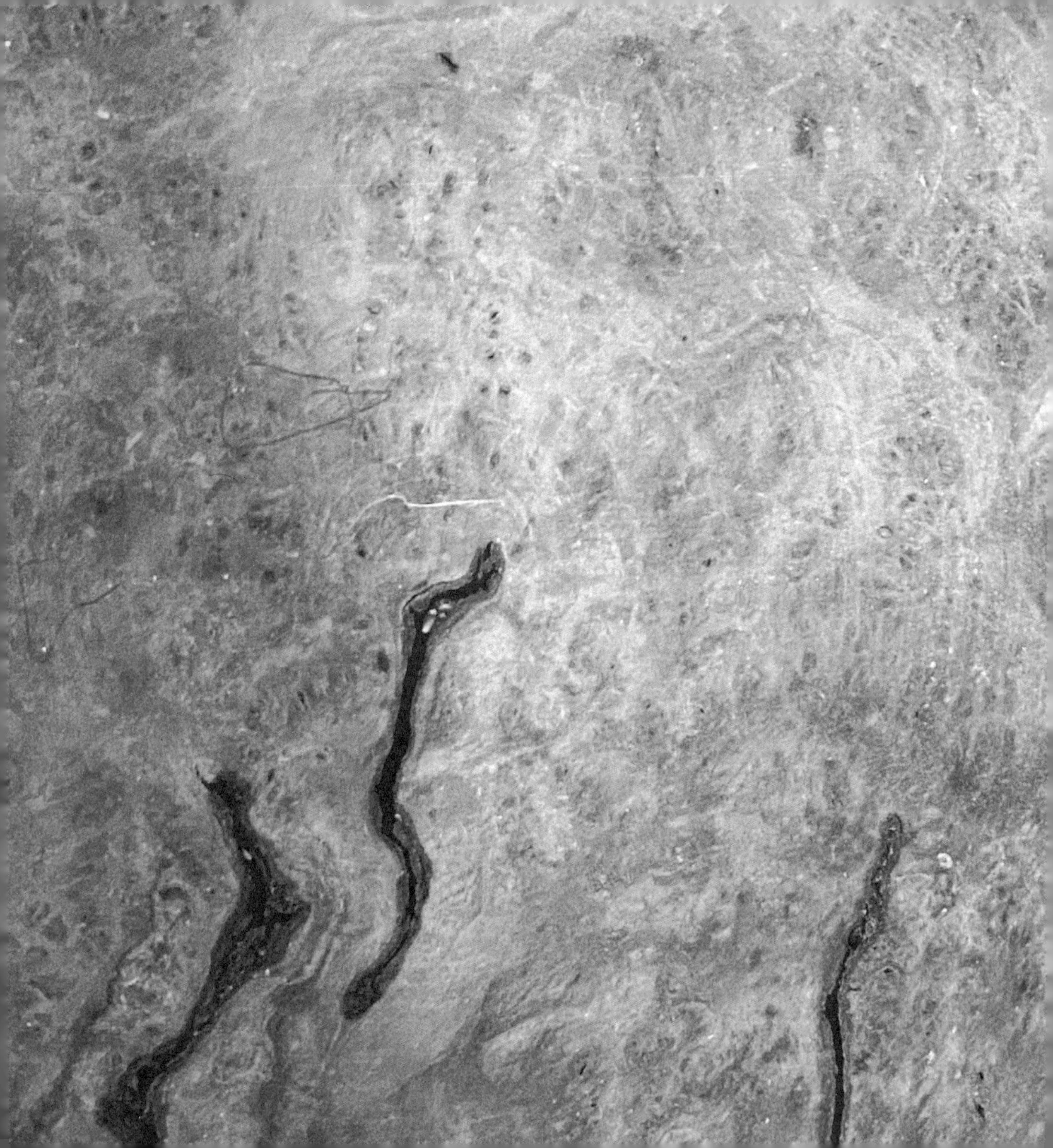

Dedicated to my children,

May you always find Him to be
Immanuel, God with you,
as you go throughout your days.

Introduction

I once read that if you want your writing to have the biggest impact you must write smaller. The smallest writing with the most intimate of details will make the biggest impact on the reader, and that is what this book is about.

We can talk about God and His greatness and His immense love for all the world, but that conversation will always keep us far from a God who longs to be up close. He wants the world, but His heart is more intricately set on you and I.

In the vastness of this millennium old religion and the machine that has become modern Christianity, a deeper reality that we often miss is that our omniscient and omnipresent God can only have the interactions with us that we give Him. We tend to think He has everything, and yet He has allowed Himself the desire to be with us and then placed the power to give or deny it in our hands. There's only one you and there's only one me, and He longs to enter into moments and interactions and relationship with each of us. But He can only have as big a relationship as we are willing to give Him.

The conversations we are willing to have with Him, the depths we are willing to go with Him, the time we are willing to give Him, the pain we hold out and share with Him— these are all within our own power and choosing.

My hope is that this book of meditations gives language to the intimate interactions we have with our Maker. How we think about Him and how He thinks about us and what it looks like when those two intentions play out in real time—in the here and now. What keeps you from Him? Where are the places you're afraid to go with Him? What do you believe about Him, and what does He believe about you?

The meditations in this book are an invitation into a deeper relationship with God. They aren't meant to be read all at one time or even in a particular order. They are individual meditations to sit with one moment at a time. And my hope is that that when you enter in to worship, to pray, to have a conversation with God or ask Him a question, that you would remember you are offering Him a gift only you can give—a unique relationship with just you. It's the smallest details we offer out that make the biggest impact on the heart of God.

May our kingdoms fall so that Yours will come,

and give us the grace to let them go.

He's made Himself known—

Across epochs

Across ages

He's made Himself known,

And here in this moment in time, He's asking to be found.

A Treasure set in our midst for such a time as this,

Could it be we're the generation who resists?

The infinite God entering finite time to know and be known by humankind,

And He asks us to steward well what we've been given—

A momentary convening with the God of Heaven.

Because to know Him here is to know Him there,

And it's important what our souls find most familiar

Will Heaven seem new?

Will God be too?

Or will we know well the face and place of our Savior?

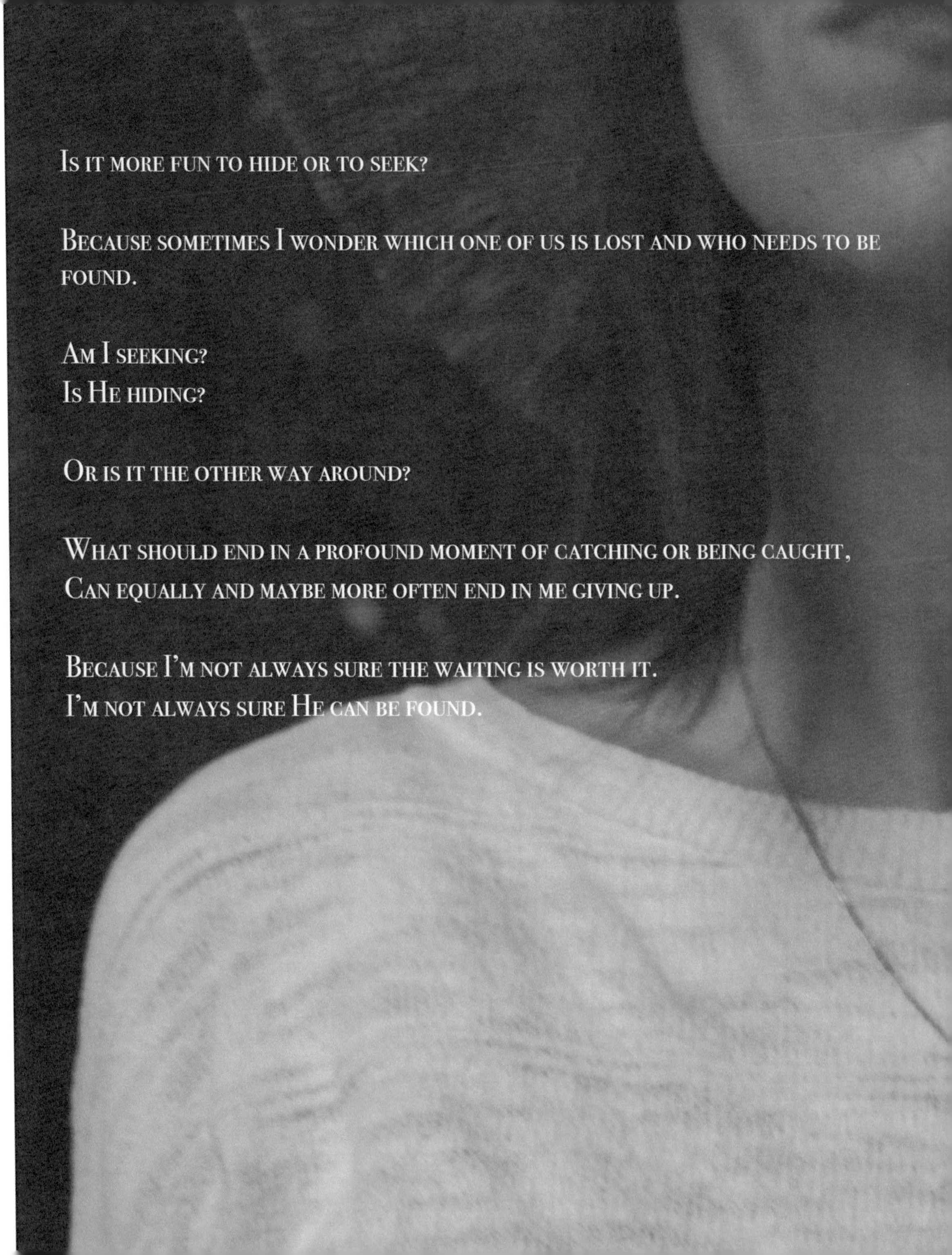

Is it more fun to hide or to seek?

Because sometimes I wonder which one of us is lost and who needs to be found.

Am I seeking?
Is He hiding?

Or is it the other way around?

What should end in a profound moment of catching or being caught,
Can equally and maybe more often end in me giving up.

Because I'm not always sure the waiting is worth it.
I'm not always sure He can be found.

Yet He promises He is the finder of lost things
The rewarder of those who seek.

So, I pick the game back up again
Try for another day.

Even if only to discover which one of us is it,
And to remember how it feels just to play.

And then maybe it was this—our mistake being
We considered Him most fragile,
Like a glass doll set upon a shelf,
Something to be displayed but never played.

But He's more real and more tangible than we've ever given Him credit for,
And He stands in radiant invitation asking us to come—
With all questions and doubts, all disagreements, and especially disappointments.

He isn't too fragile for our real and every day life,
And most importantly, our friendship isn't too fragile either.

So, He beckons us to come closer,
Come challenge what might stand between us.

Because He values us more than the outcome.
He values our communion with one another more than whatever our rigid faith might stand to offer.

And so, we come.

Hands full and hearts full of all the unpacking this life gives in turn,
And He smiles as He tells us about Himself, about ourselves, and about a kingdom for which we yearn.

We wake to a whisper that calls us out of bed

before the alarms and sleepy kids

and rush of this time-held life we tread.

He calls to say—

Come start your day in peace.

Come rise with me instead of rising

to all the things you have to do.

Come feel the stillness

that makes no demand of you

Come be with me.

When we bring our truest selves, He offers back His true self.
Unmarred and untainted, He shows Himself as He is,
And not as we perceive Him to be.

But it takes us showing up with an offering of authenticity.

This is who I am,

This is what I've done,

And I've brought it here.

And it feels like a trade. A bargaining game.

But isn't that how friendships are made?

A vulnerability,

A deeper intimacy,

A self offered bits at a time to be reciprocated in kind.

And we can bet He knows best how to play.

Always overmatching our underachieving and offering an upgrade.

Show Me your weakness I'll show you My strength.
Share your doubts, and I'll give you back faith.
Tell Me your fears and Love you will find.
Whisper your secrets, I'll whisper back Mine.

He gives beyond measure. His reward is full.
It just takes showing up in His throne room without pretense or bull...

He finds us.
In carved out moments planned before time,
He finds us.

His glory,
His story,
Being God with us.

He comes
to tell us His story
in real time,

God with us in the here and now—

A narrative of the Divine.

The present holds His presence,

and before we even look we find ourselves running.

We run from moments towards future ones

hoping they hold a better gift,

and we miss that the here and now

is what builds heart space and equips.

Missing this means missing Him,

And our lives weren't made to be skimmed.

So, we try to walk slowly
try to tread lightly
entering into moments of now,
to find Him there illuminating all that is poignant and profound.
He waits for us in time-filled moments
hoping we'll wait for Him.
He has things to say
a love that's great
and a greater grace yet to be found.

DAILY STOIC

Maybe He's always there
Always there waiting.

For the turn of our head,
For a whisper from our heart,
For our truest selves to show up in His throne room.

He's always there waiting.

Waiting for us to come as we are so we can interact with who He is—
Without pretense or perfection,
Without façade or our fictional selves,

Just us,
And just Him,

Like old friends walking in the Garden again.

Stepping into gratitude is like stepping into sunlight–

He meets us there.

It's common ground

A halfway point

The boundary between dark and light.

Gratitude is our aptitude for seeing in the night.

And there He stands in meeting

Marking paths to lead the way,

Our awareness ever growing

Of the goodness He has laid.

Our gratitude an offering

And yet a doorway all the same,

It breaks through what lies around us

Into a place of endless grace.

Sometimes, we find ourselves needy—spiritually poor
And in asking for relief, we find there isn't room for more.
Our souls have filled up with other things
Shrunken down to a lesser capacity.

We wonder why He doesn't answer—why He won't give.
We assume He's the issue in this place where we live.

But His hand's never lacking, it doesn't fall short.
He's abundantly giving grace of all sorts.

So, we ask not what we can get, but what we must give away,
Of the vices and gluttonous sins that stand in our way.

And He bends low to speak with a smile on His face—
For giving graces and goodness isn't all that He seeks.
He seeks us and us wholly, without pretense or posture,
When questions are asked, relationships get fostered.

He withholds promises as we await their arrival, because He's growing something deeper.
His whispered promise falls deep into our hearts and grows in our soul
as we anticipate the outcome.
A word given yet delayed in fruition.

And we rest.

Like Abraham waiting for his son to be born.
Like Joseph waiting for his chains to be torn.
Like David waiting for his kingship restored.

Men who were built upon the word of God because they endured the time of their missing promise.
They overcame and they became, and the promise fulfilled proved them all men able to stand under the weight their promise held.
So, we wait for our promises.
Becoming and overcoming,
Forging ourselves along the way,
Until we learn to grow into His last promise given–
I will be with you even to the end, hold on and be ready, I'm coming back again.

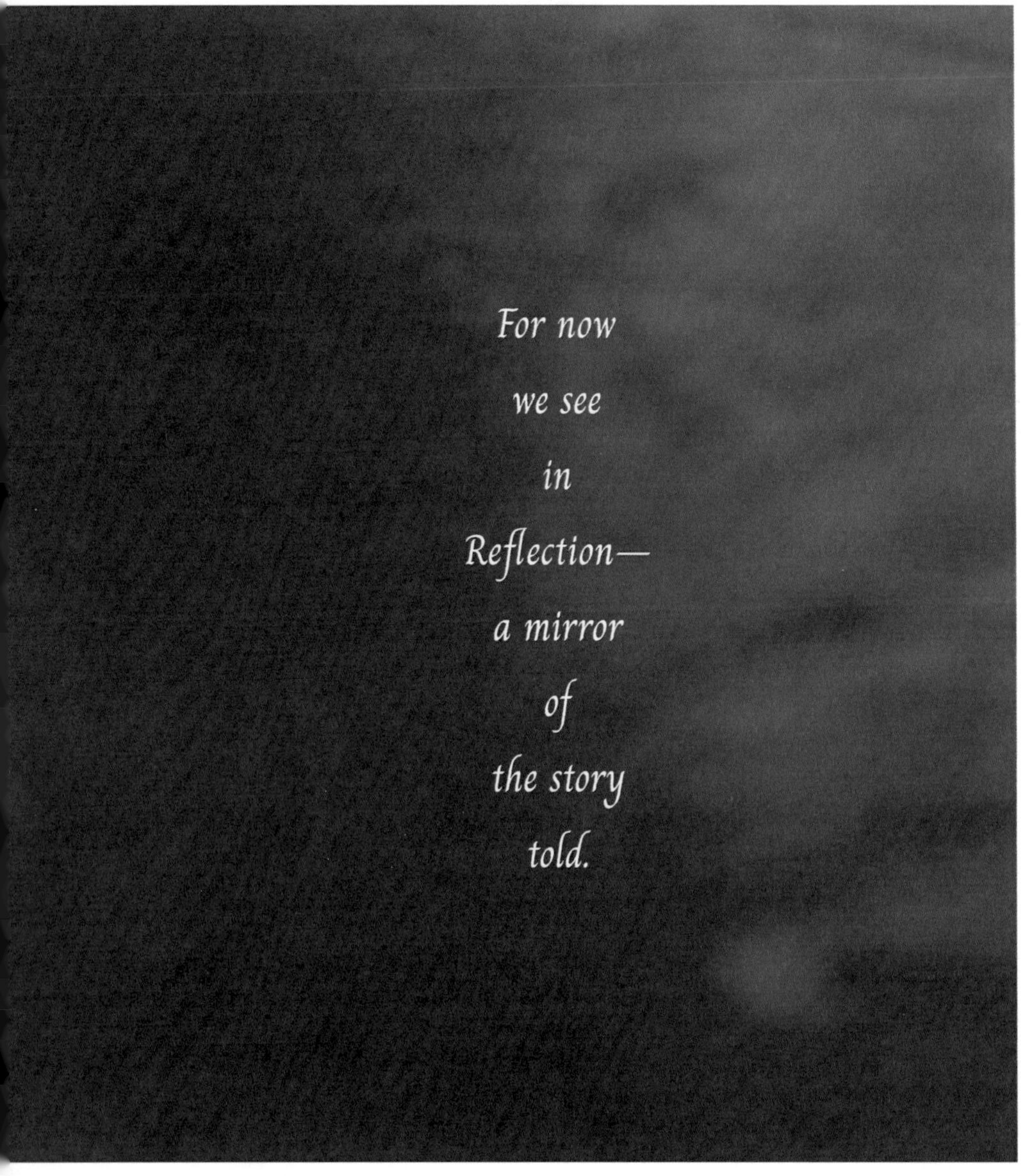

For now

we see

in

Reflection—

a mirror

of

the story

told.

But one day—face to face.

Face to face with the Son of Man
Face to face with the Great I AM

Face to face—

As He originally planned.

There is a glory in moving towards Him when we are still shrouded in darkness.
When we do not feel His nearness,
When sin has cloaked our way,
When brokenness leaves us in broken pieces,
And wholeness stretches arm's lengths away.
There's an offering that only then we can give,
From hearts that have hardened and souls rent like sieves.
For though we feel Him not, our faith still stands
In the bowing of posture and raising of hands.
To turn towards the Light when darkness holds fast,
Is to testify to Truth when all evidence looks bad.
Only we can do it
And only in this place
Of broken things and wayward wishes
The prodigal remembering God's face.

THE SPIRITUALLY POOR
ARE THE POOR IN SPIRIT,
AND WE FORGET
THAT THE KINGDOM OF HEAVEN
BELONGS TO SUCH AS THESE.

HE'S THE REDEEMER OF ALL THINGS,
RESTORING ALL THAT WE BRING,
TRADING BEAUTY FOR ASHES,
AND STILL WE WONDER
WHY WE SIT WITH
BROKEN WINGS.

And we give things up for Him, because He's worth knowing,
Worth clearing the path for.

Worth rearranging our lives a bit so we can see Him more clearly, Hear Him more succinctly.

He's promised to reward those who seek Him,
And we bank on that promise coming true,

Bank on Him showing up if we do.

It's an act of faith that brings about His promises,
So, we lay our things down trusting –

That if we seek, we will find

If we ask, He'll prove Himself kind

If we run after Him, we'll find Him sprinting our way–
Arm's open wide.

Sacrifice and offerings are always a conversation piece between us and God.

Always relational

Always a move of friendship and never because He's conditional.

There we sat and there He was–

A Whisper

A Grace

A Love

He comes in unassuming, only whispering His truths.

He's barely above notice in crowded, loud rooms.

But that is His game, brilliantly played.
The ones who can hear Him hold all else at bay.
So we bow down to listen, quiet our souls,
For our King speaks softly wherever He goes.
Sober in spirit, vices laid rest,
A steadied heart waiting under quiet arrest.

We do not fear darkness itself. We fear darkness because in it we cannot see, in it, we do not know.

But what if in the midst of darkness LIGHT begins to dawn, and we see things we've never seen before— understand things we've never known before?

What then?

Sometimes we play in the hallway of the setting sun to catch the last rays because we fear so much the darkness beyond the threshold of a place we've never known.

And we wait out an invitation long past due because we're afraid—afraid He won't meet us in that unlit room.

But He is calling.

Calling us to come see,

Calling us to come know,

Calling us into deeper friendship with Him.

For once the darkness begins to settle and our weak eyes begin to see untold treasures of God Himself—all missed—because of a place we feared to be.

We wake for this moment of meeting expecting to find Him,
Himself given,
Only to find He's sometimes left a letter instead.
A Word written.
And we are left to seek that which is hidden.

He's calling us out of times of meeting to tell us a better story—one of friendship,
Because a moment in the morning isn't all that He is after.

He's after you,
He's after me,

And He's hoping we will find within ourselves hearts that are after Him.

Meet Me in the morning, He says, but find me in all the moments yet to be.
Walk with Me. Talk with Me. I abide in everything you see.

And so, He hides.
Stands us up.
Plays hooky from our scheduled bind,
Because meetings are for business partners,
And He thinks friendship a better use of time.

Veiled in glory,
He reaches down to touch
Hearts made of dust.

He comes into our spaces,
Shows up in unexpected places

Invading times,

Invading kingdoms,

Invading races.

The God enthroned in glory
Who enters into all our stories,
Because it's where He's always wanted to be.

An infinite God entering time,

Dwelling in temporary design,

All so He could know us.

He finds His home here,
So we can know a home there—
Eternal and immortal in His throne room.

The God who became human
To counter our revolution,

And the King will have his reward.

Gentle and lowly,

on the broken table

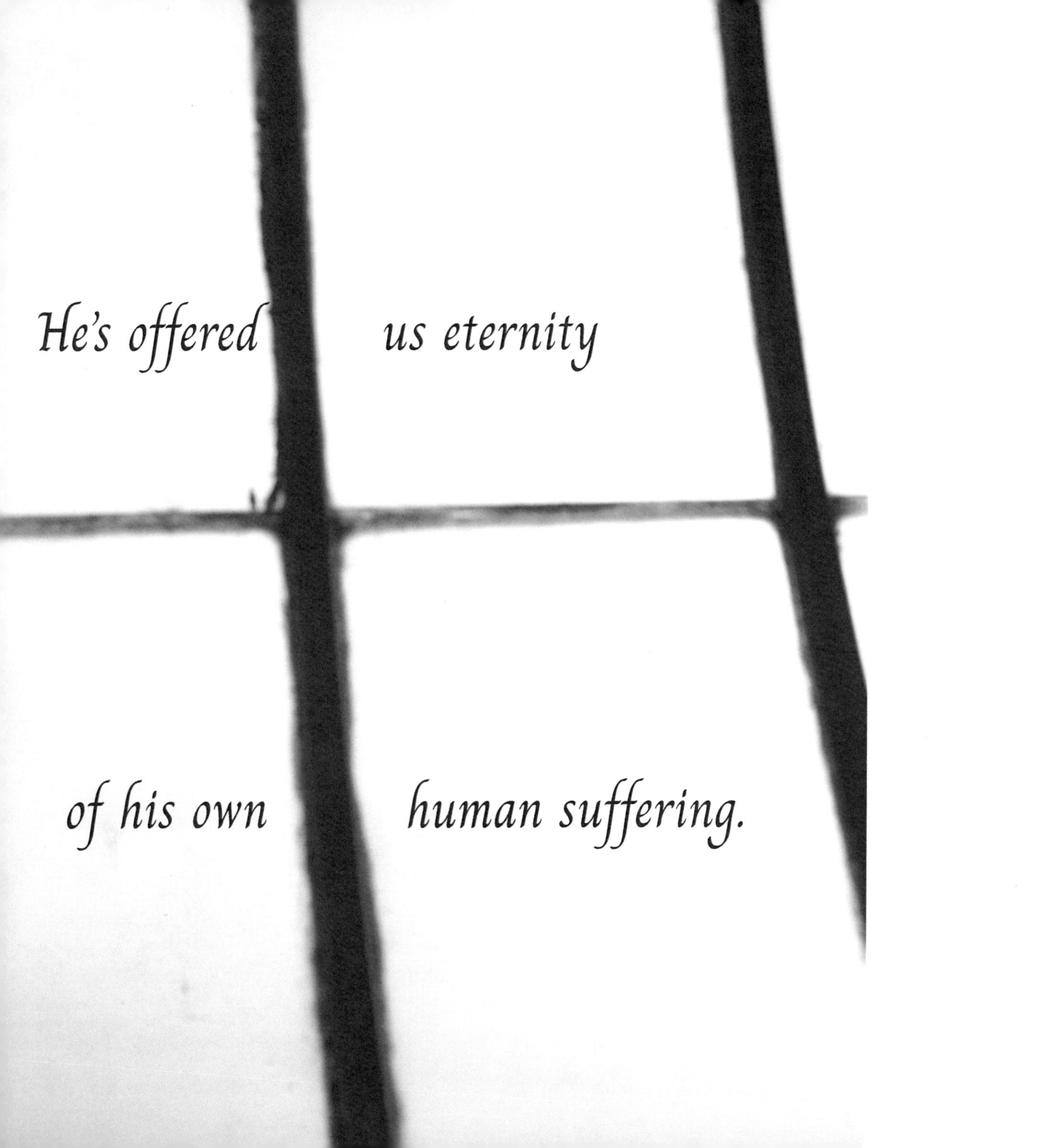

He's offered us eternity

of his own human suffering.

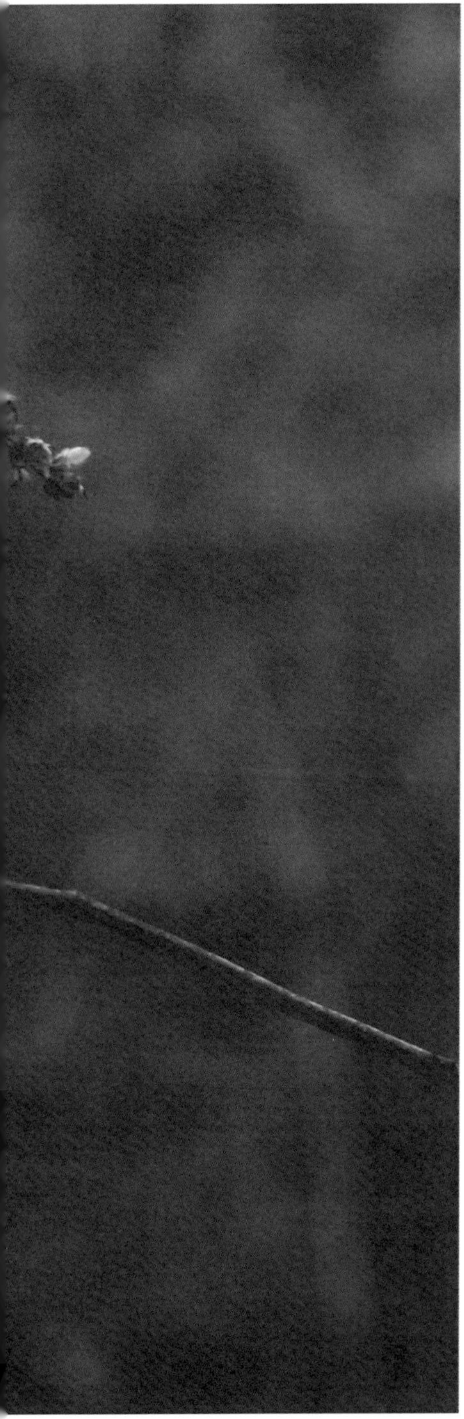

A bruised reed He will not break,

A dimly lit wick He will not extinguish,

Because He is the God who holds us by the hand

and watches over us.

The God who bends low to invite us in

and remembers that we are but dust.

He invites us back in all our fragility—

The mighty God cloaked in gentle vulnerability.

We're asking for good things as if they exist apart from the King,
And we wonder why our prayers go unanswered.

We want them without Him, and we enter in—
demanding and ill-mannered.
Give us peace, give us rest, give us hope, let us be blessed.
Take our grief, take our troubles, we want broad paths without struggle.

And we forget and have forgotten,

That He is good
That He is our rest
He is the Prince of peace for the anxious and depressed
He is wisdom
He is grace
He is mercy for the displaced
He is kindness that brings repentance
His hand reaches to befriend us

And yet we ask as if the gifts are separate from the Giver,
An inheritance taken—no relation to the Father,
We think we can have one without having the other.

And we wonder why our prayers go unanswered.

He's like a Father

Leaving gifts we had asked for but forgotten along the way.

Seamlessly they were woven in without a word,
like a breakfast table set for early morning, a new dress
hanging in the closet, or a love note dropped into an old but
well-loved book.

Gifts big and small He slips into our lives
waiting for the surprise.

And we often marvel that He doesn't show up
then and there to collect His praise.

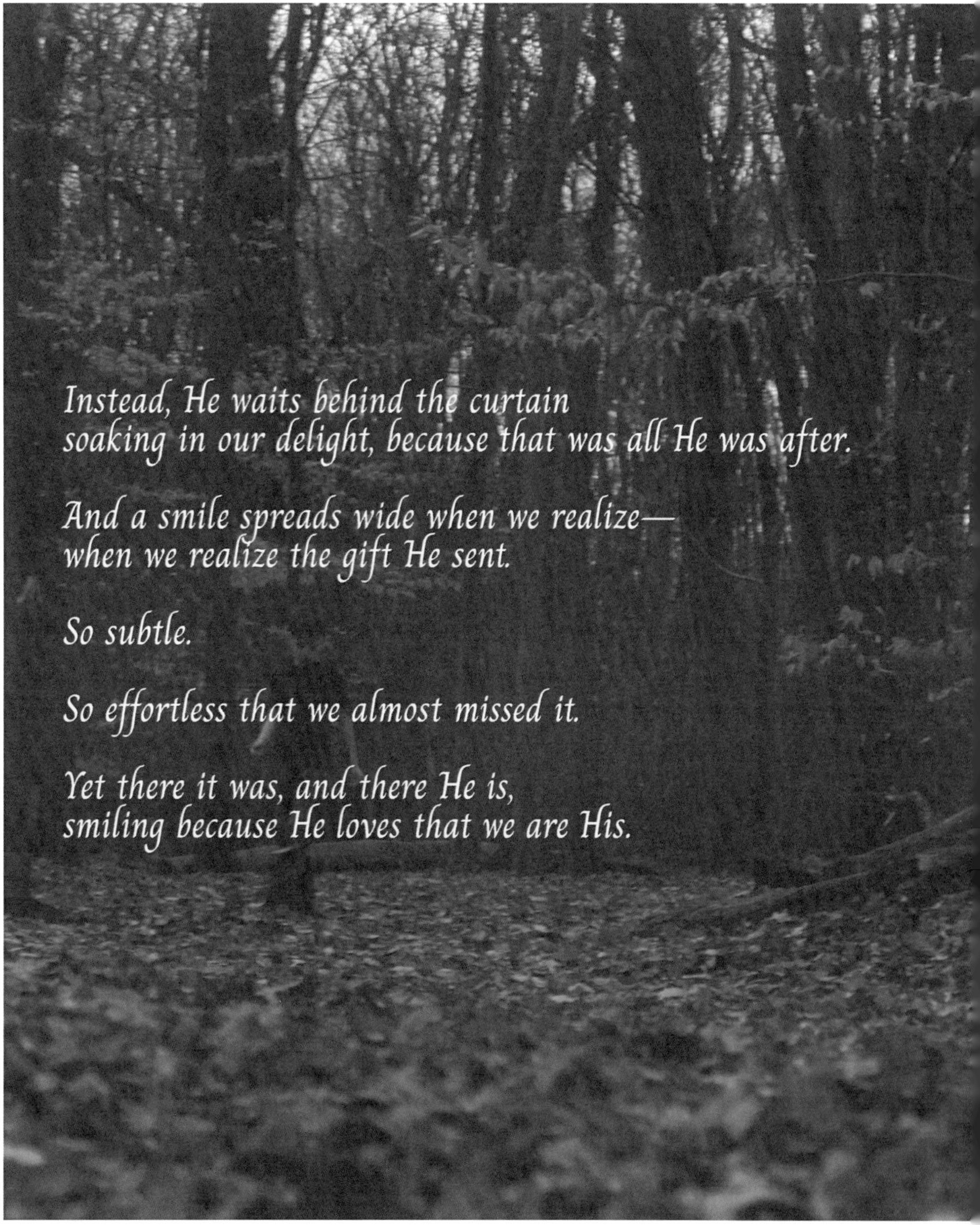

Instead, He waits behind the curtain
soaking in our delight, because that was all He was after.

And a smile spreads wide when we realize—
when we realize the gift He sent.

So subtle.

So effortless that we almost missed it.

Yet there it was, and there He is,
smiling because He loves that we are His.

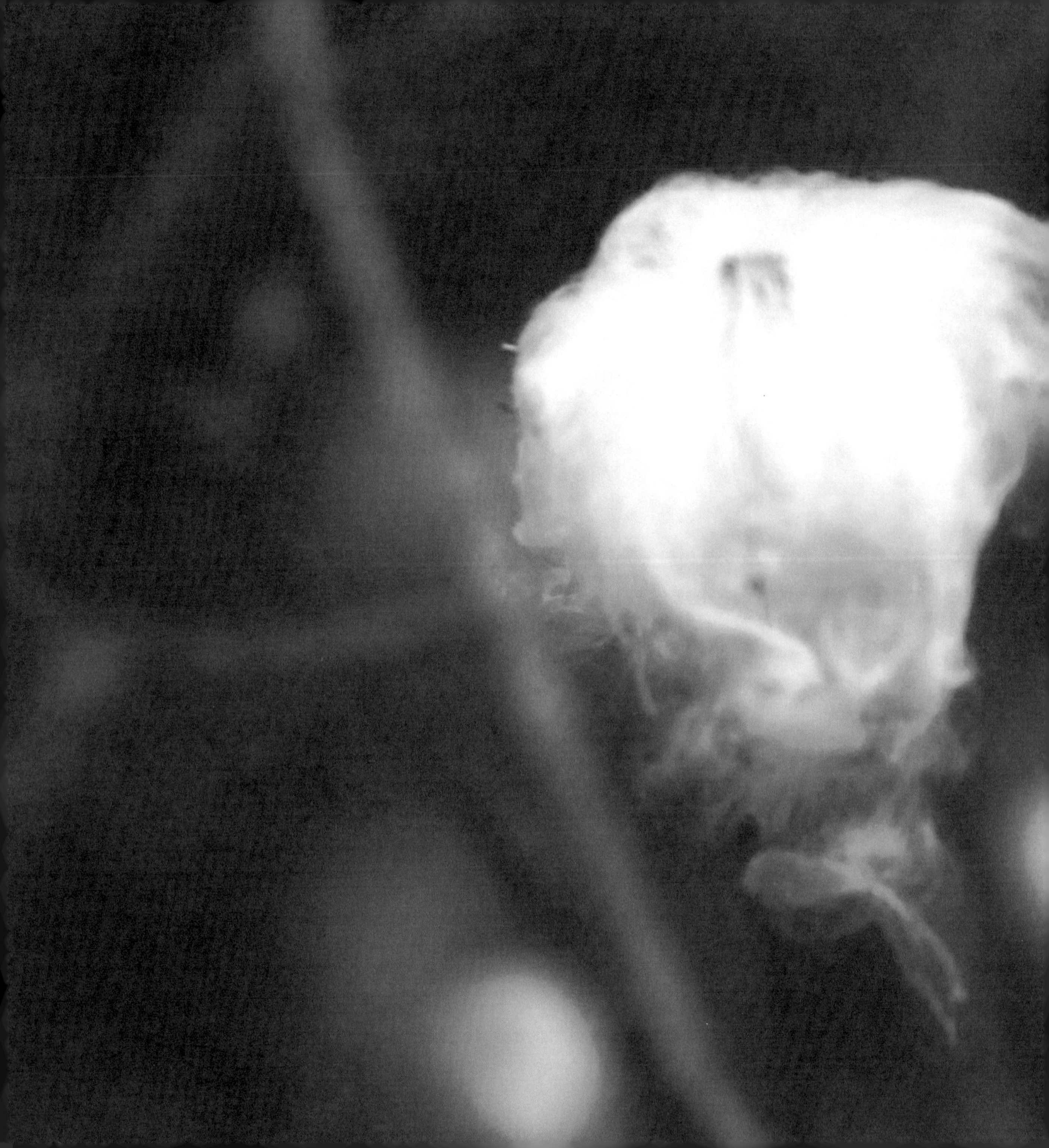

He's actively creating eternity in our midst,

Sowing seeds now to be grown and harvested for a later feast,

Eternal seeds grown in mortal ground,

And He asks if we would join His work.

His Kingdom every growing, ever working toward an end,

And He longs for us to have a portion to tend.

To tend to what we have here for an inheritance there.

He asks us to ask, so Kingdom answers can be given,

He asks us to knock, so Kingdom paths can be opened,

He asks us to seek because He knows that we'll find

All of Heaven open—an inheritance given in kind.

One day we'll stumble upon the beautiful things we left behind, things too wonderful that we stored them away for safe keeping, and there we forgot them.

Then comes a time where we find something old and see it with new eyes, new hope, and we might be told by those of old that it's past its time and no longer useful, but we must always remember:

He is redeeming all things.

He is restoring all things.

What rusty and broken down things we might find in the pages we've left behind—they're just in need of a little oil.

To be taken out and played with again,

Paper meeting pen again,

Stepping out in faith again,

He breathes new life where we ask Him.

Sometimes,

things seem dark,

because

He's directing us

to where

the

light falls.

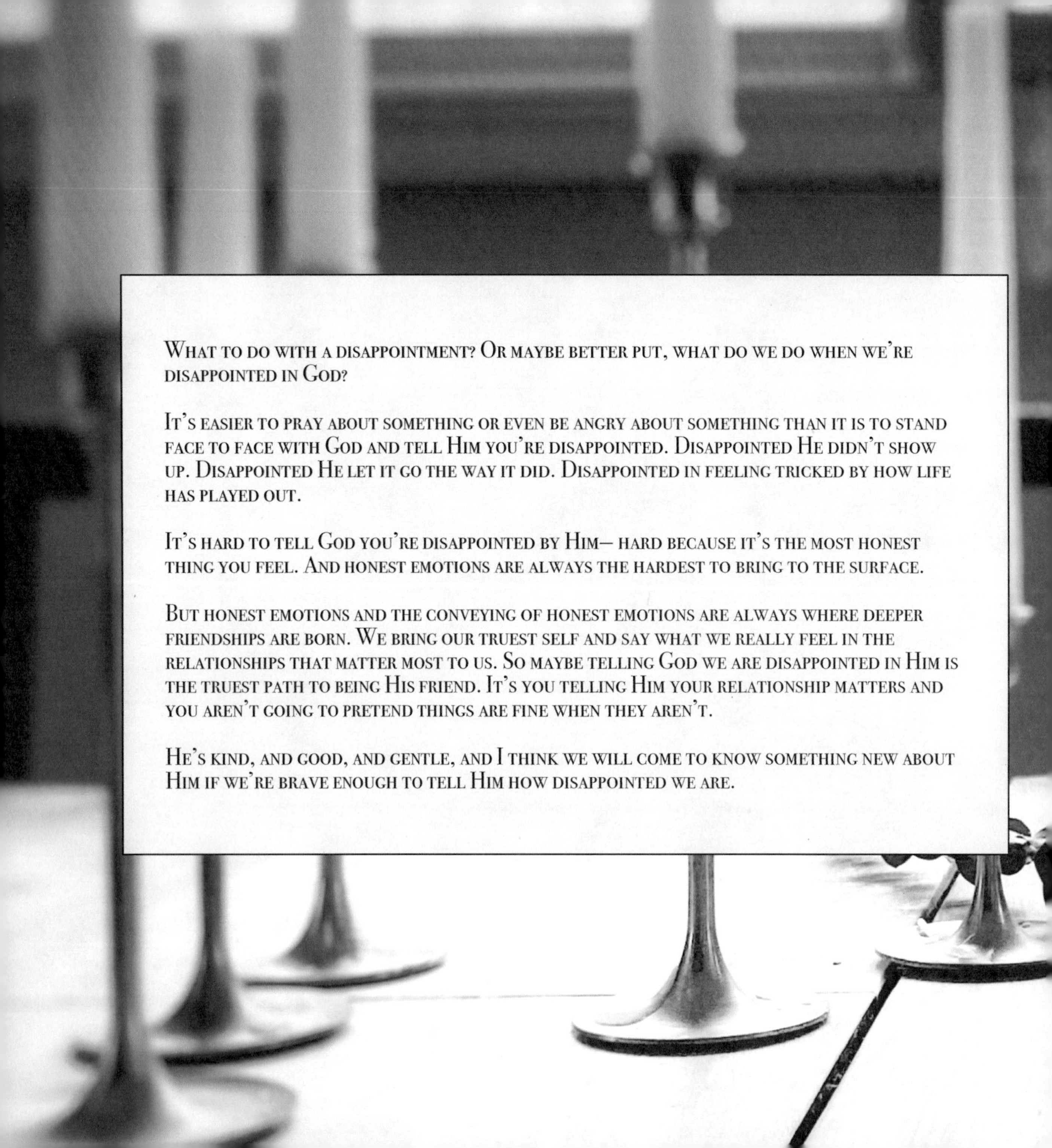

What to do with a disappointment? Or maybe better put, what do we do when we're disappointed in God?

It's easier to pray about something or even be angry about something than it is to stand face to face with God and tell Him you're disappointed. Disappointed He didn't show up. Disappointed He let it go the way it did. Disappointed in feeling tricked by how life has played out.

It's hard to tell God you're disappointed by Him— hard because it's the most honest thing you feel. And honest emotions are always the hardest to bring to the surface.

But honest emotions and the conveying of honest emotions are always where deeper friendships are born. We bring our truest self and say what we really feel in the relationships that matter most to us. So maybe telling God we are disappointed in Him is the truest path to being His friend. It's you telling Him your relationship matters and you aren't going to pretend things are fine when they aren't.

He's kind, and good, and gentle, and I think we will come to know something new about Him if we're brave enough to tell Him how disappointed we are.

SterlingPro

There once was a man after God's own heart who stood before a giant. We would do well to consider him often.

How he stood before Goliath not because he could, but because he had a promise that said he would be king. A promise from a prophet whose word had never once fallen.

What a thing to stand on.
What a thing to face a giant with.

A word always proven to be true.

And yet here we stand, today, on promises from a God who promised His word will never return to Him void—a word greater than Samuel.

A word that promises we will find Him if we seek Him.

A word that promises grace and mercy in time of need.

A word that promises Himself always, here with us, even 'til the end of age.

Ask and it will be given you.

And we're reminded often that it is us who have underestimated God and His promise and not God who has come short on the word He has given.

Heaven's calling.

To all who stand on the sandy beaches of life's carefully crafted sandcastles,
A deeper invitation has gone out.

It calls, a kingdom coming,
Asking us to join ranks before it arrives,

"Keep building sandcastles or come out where waters thrive.

Come out beyond your own understanding
Where faith keeps you afloat;
Come wade into waters moving in rhythms lost but no longer remote.
Come out past shallow lives ruined by the tide,
For all that can be shaken will be taken in stride.
Come swim out past waves and whirlpools
Into dark and steady waters,
Where the Whisper of the One safely keeps—

It's deep calling out to deep.

Where you lose your life confined to ground
To one with breadth and width and depth
And movement all around."

His kingdom reveals itself in proportion to our affections for it.
It's as near to us as our awareness is to it.

Like a photographer taking a photograph,
Seeing the picture before it's taken,
We see His kingdom before it comes
Because our hearts were set on waiting.

Waiting for His kingdom and not our own,
Knowing something greater could be shown.

And this is how we bring His kingdom:

Like a picture born through the one who sees what is not,
Our affections and awareness set on what the world forgot.

His kingdom, visible to and born through those who diligently look for its arrival,
Already aware, actively prepared, with a lens focused and open for revival.

Photo by Ingrid Frankovics

Currently living in Michigan with her husband and three children, Kelly Meagher is a writer and poet who has endlessly pursued the intersection of where God's Kingdom meets the world's most broken places. In her pursuit, she has found God's goodness to be an unimaginably powerful force of healing. With a passion to spread a new way of looking at and understanding God's goodness, Kelly writes inspirational narratives and prose to draw others into a new way of living in relationship with God and His Kingdom.

Connect with Kelly on Instagram:
@kellyannemeagher

Printed in the USA
CPSIA information can be obtained
at www.ICGtesting.com
LVRC101144060124
768169LV00024B/976

9781088033937